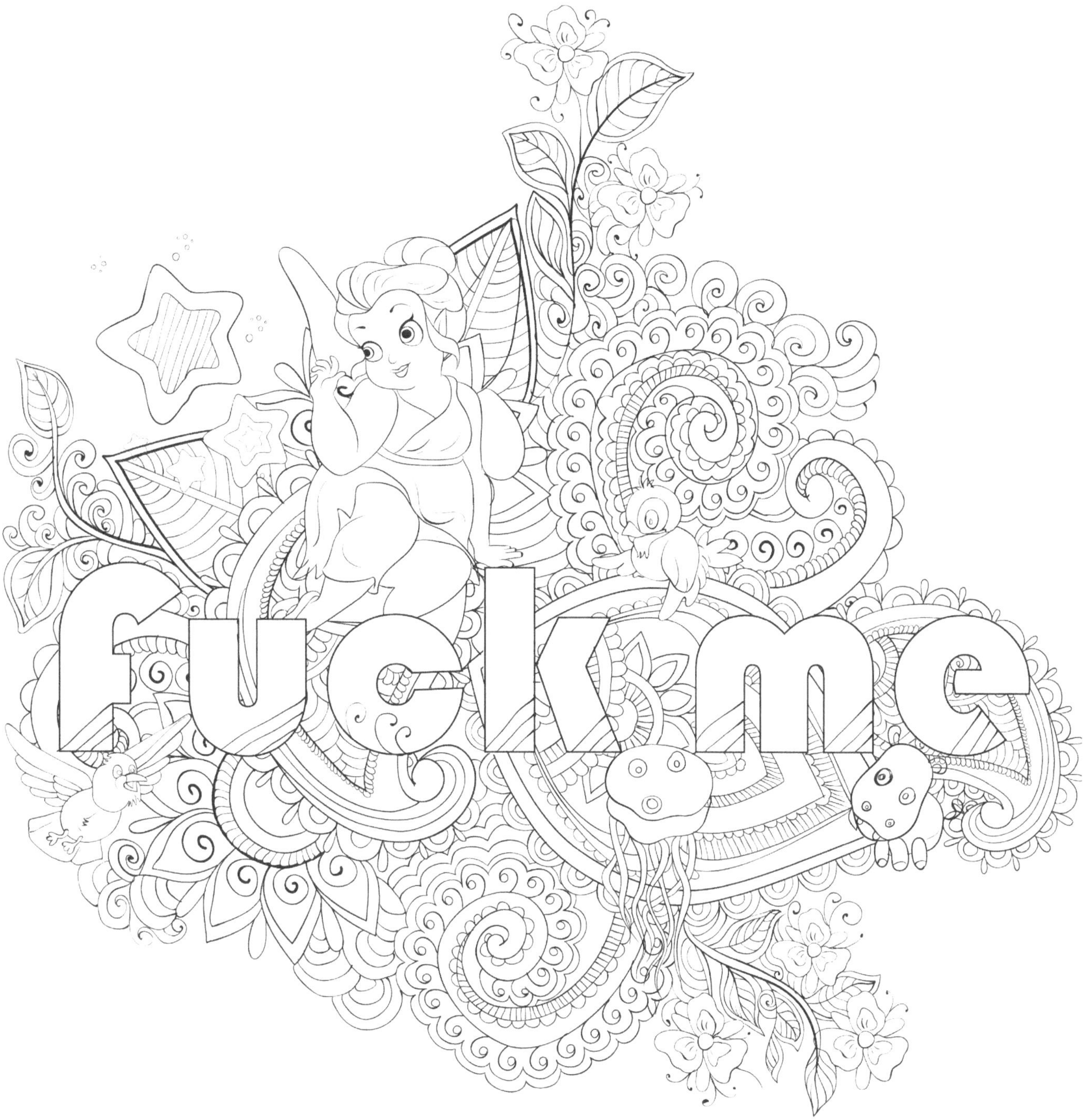

ISBN: 978-1523957767

By Artists:
    Mandala & Caricature Illustration
    Joshua Lazana Lagman and Jade Villaremo
Art Director: lluontheloose

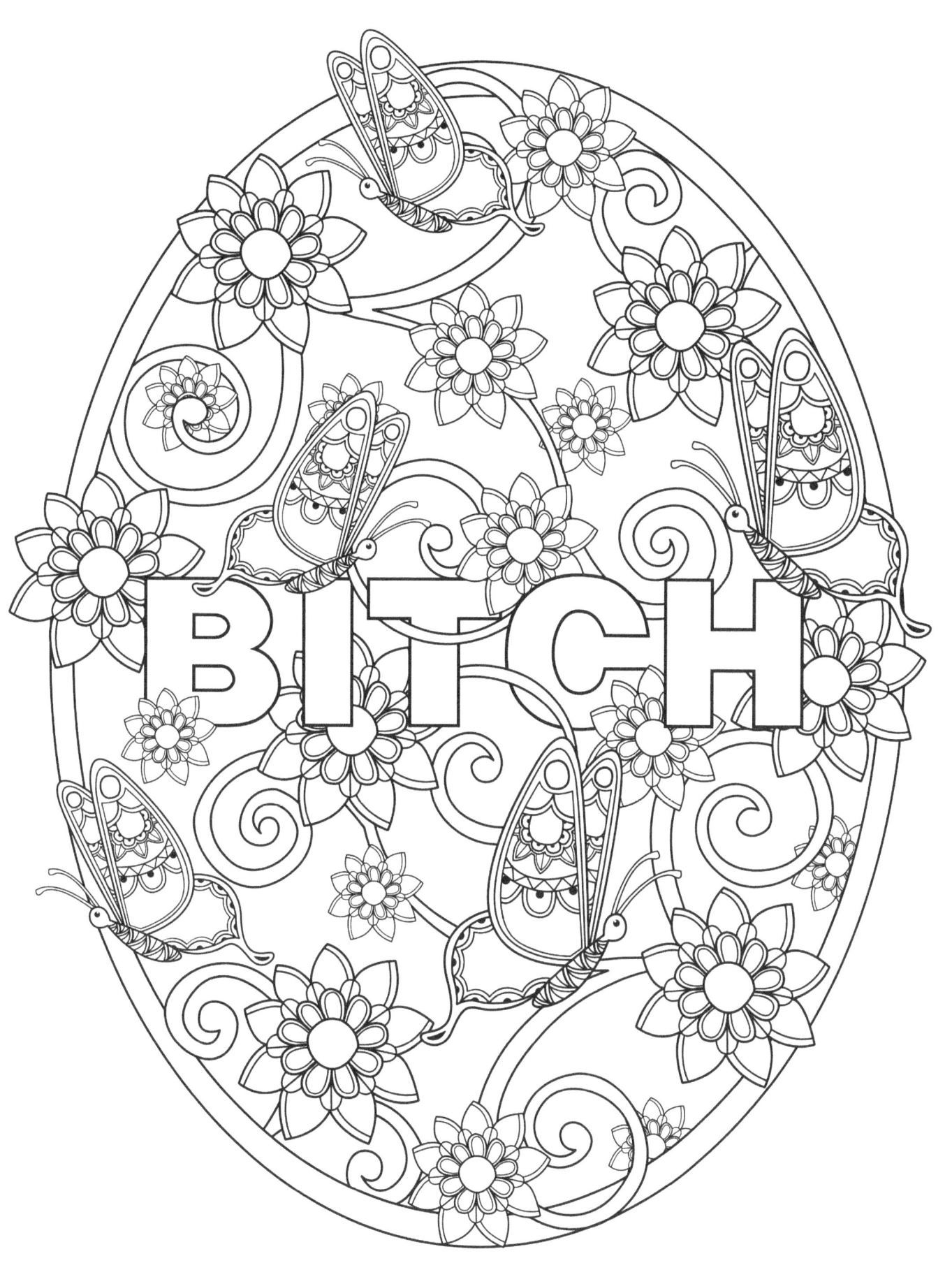

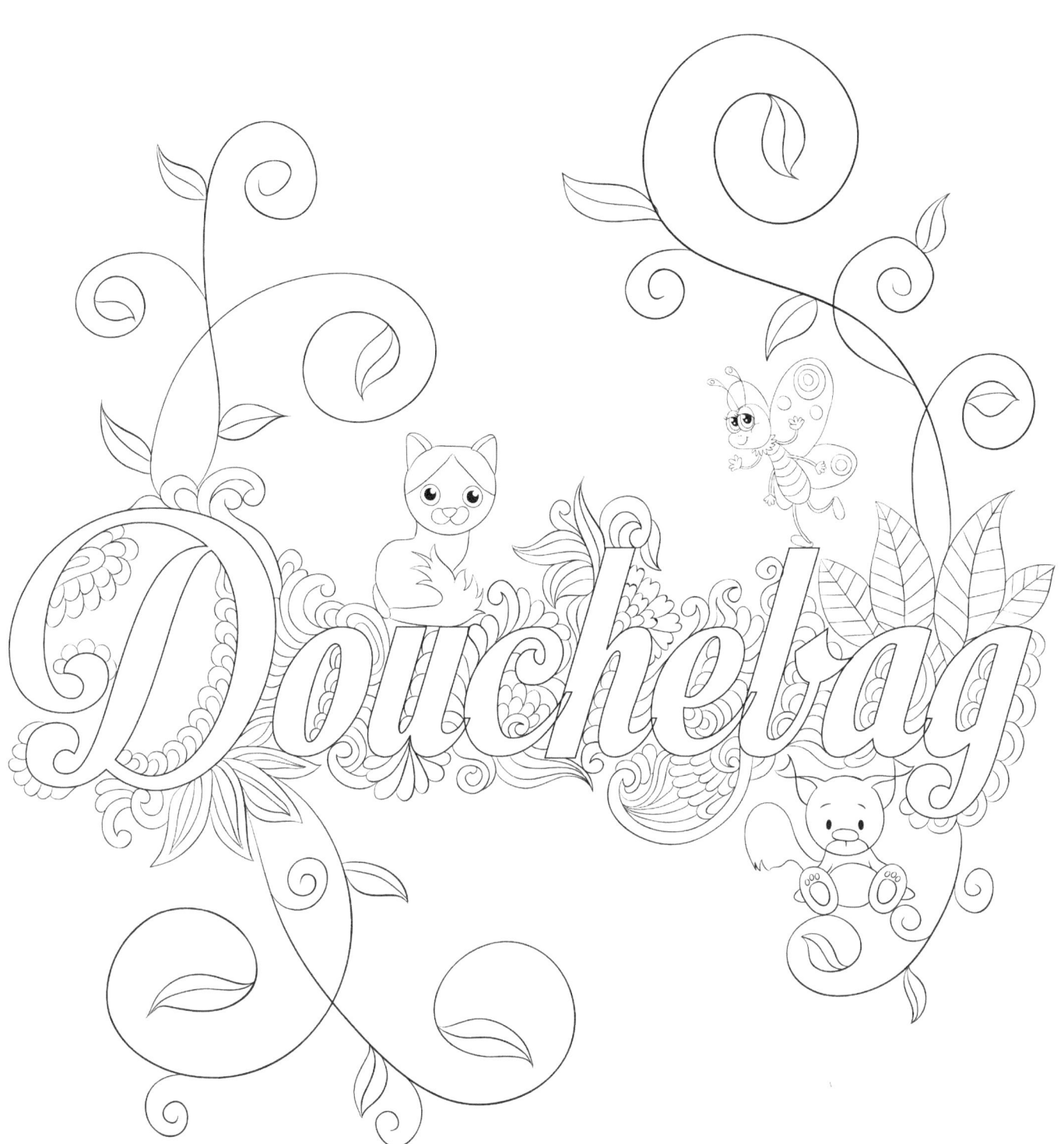

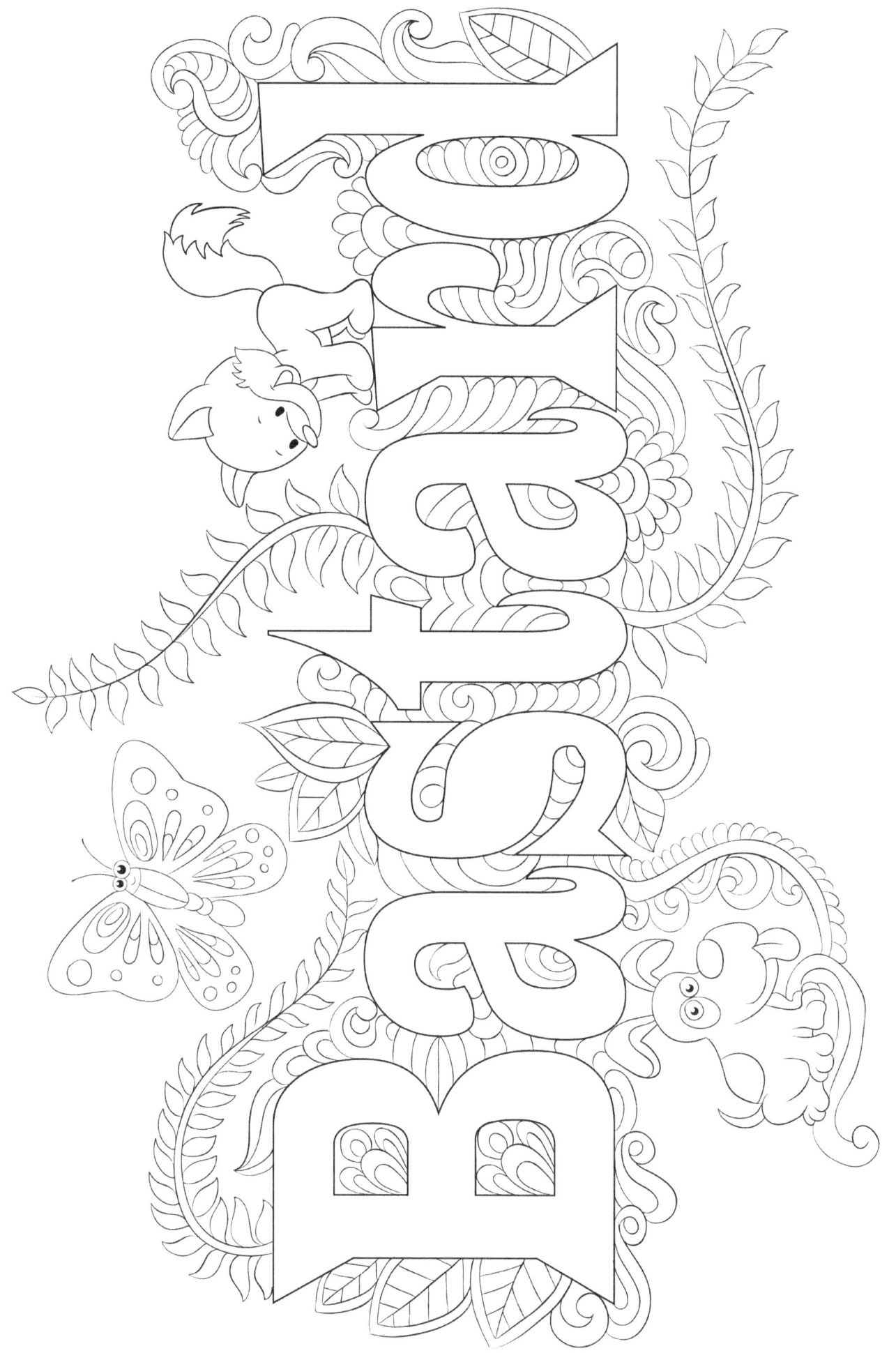

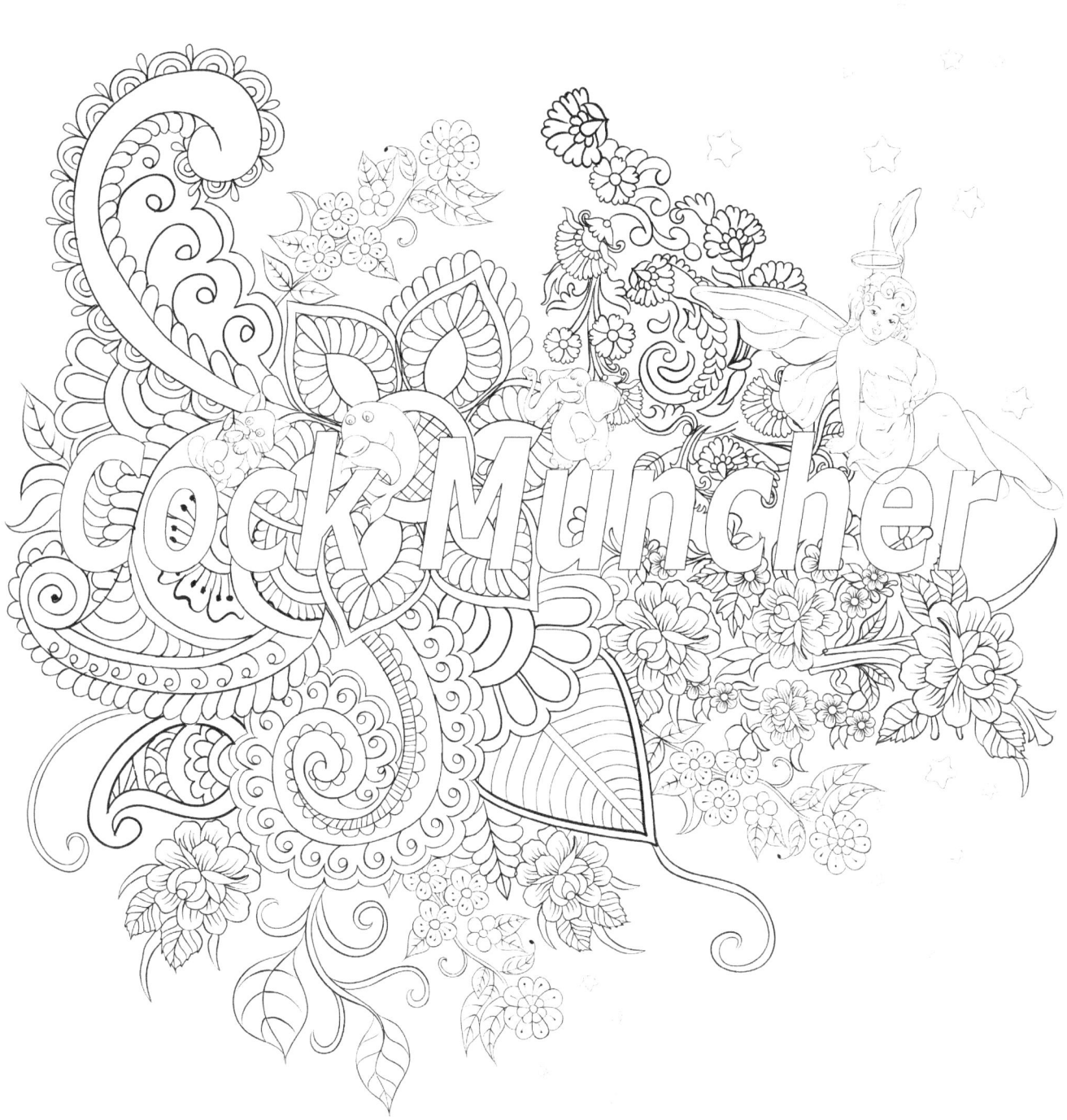

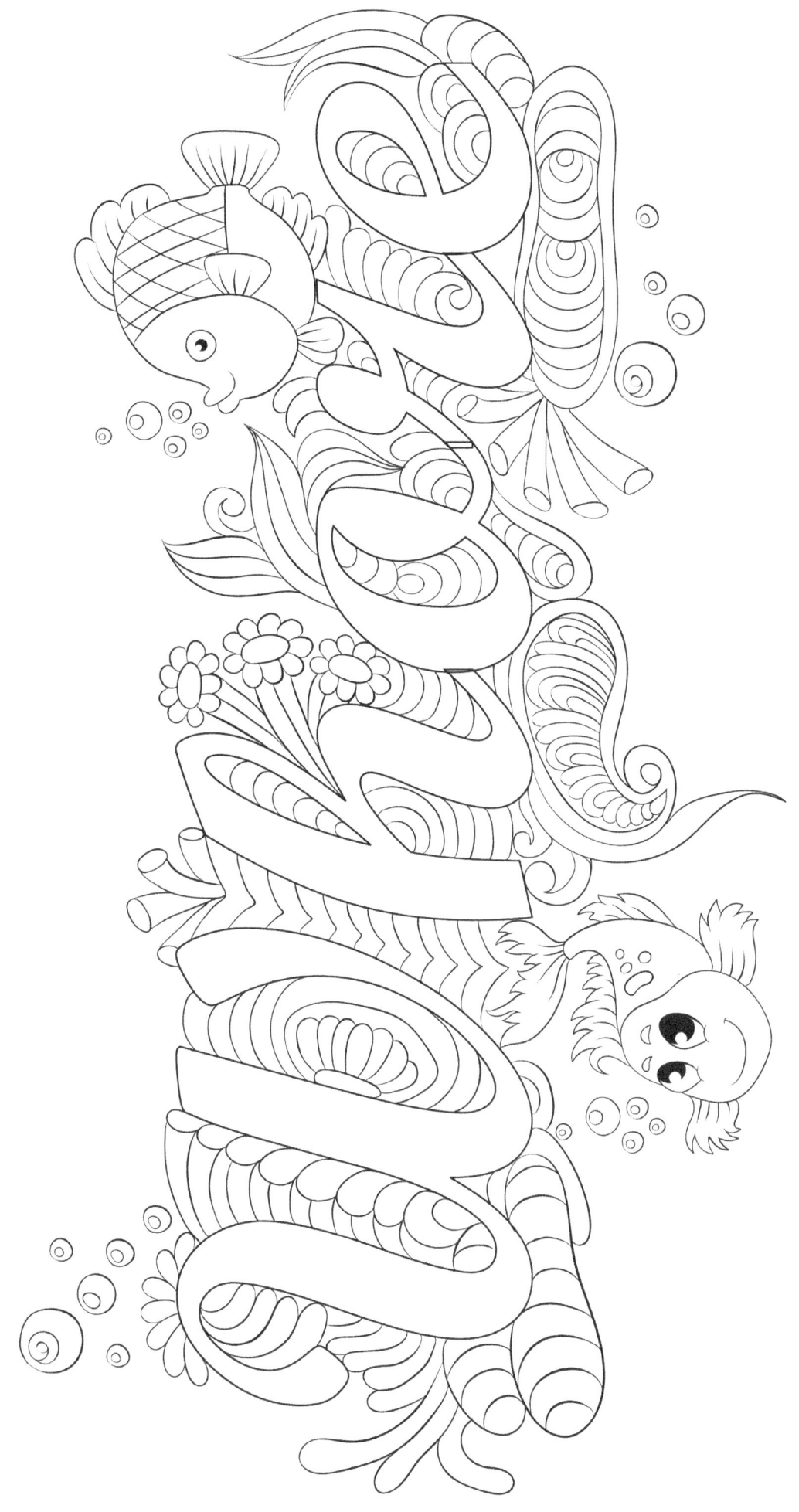

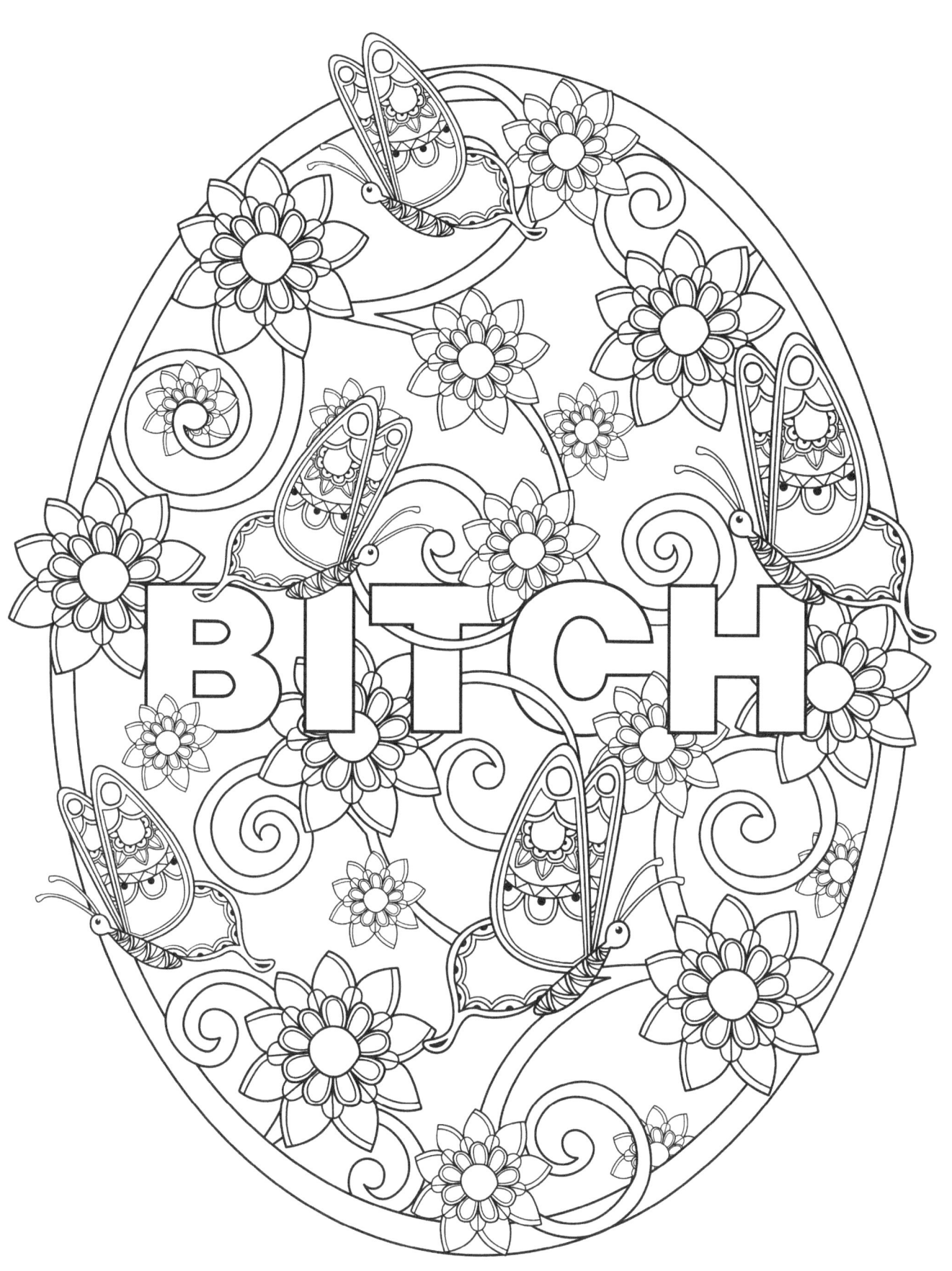

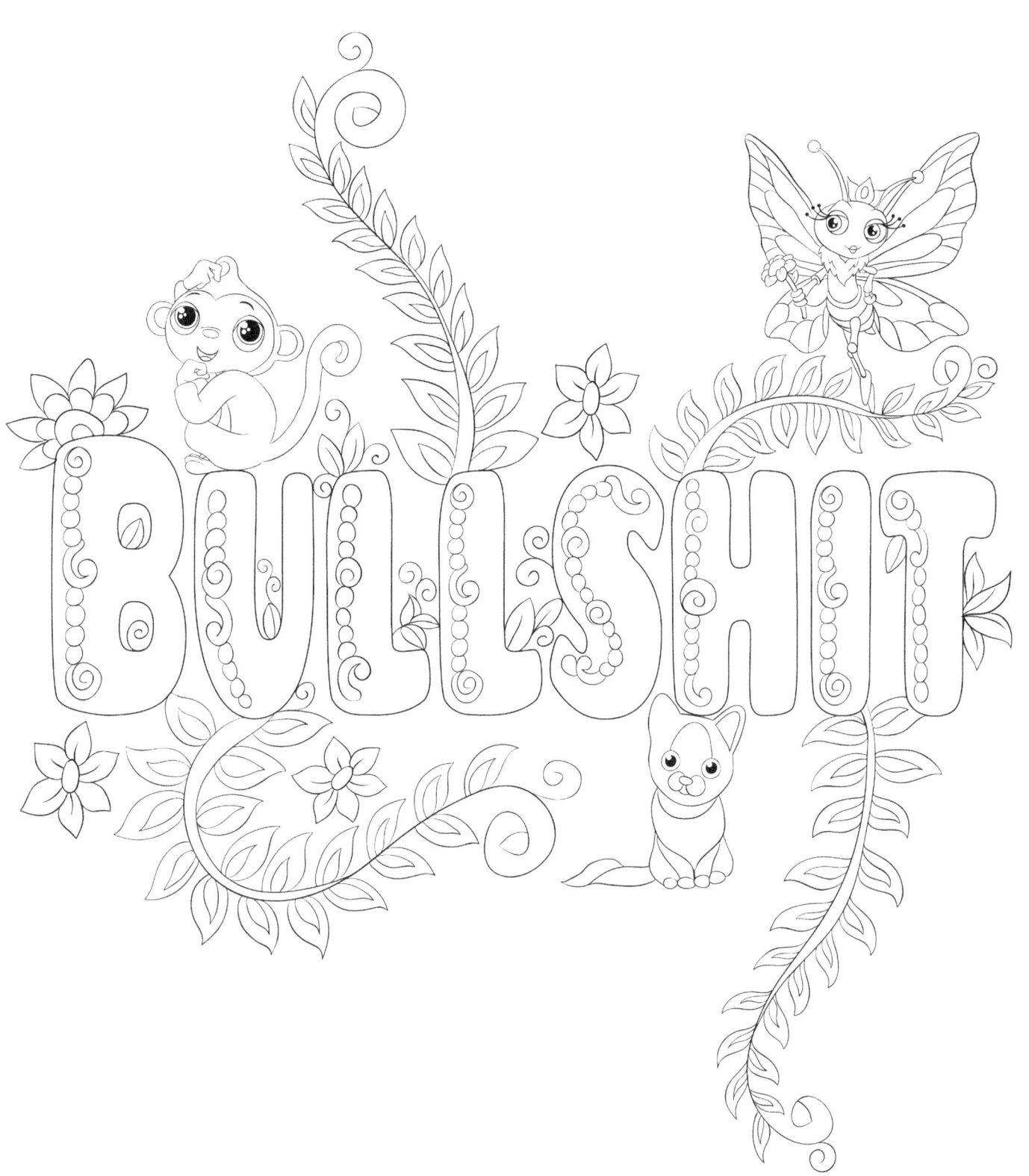

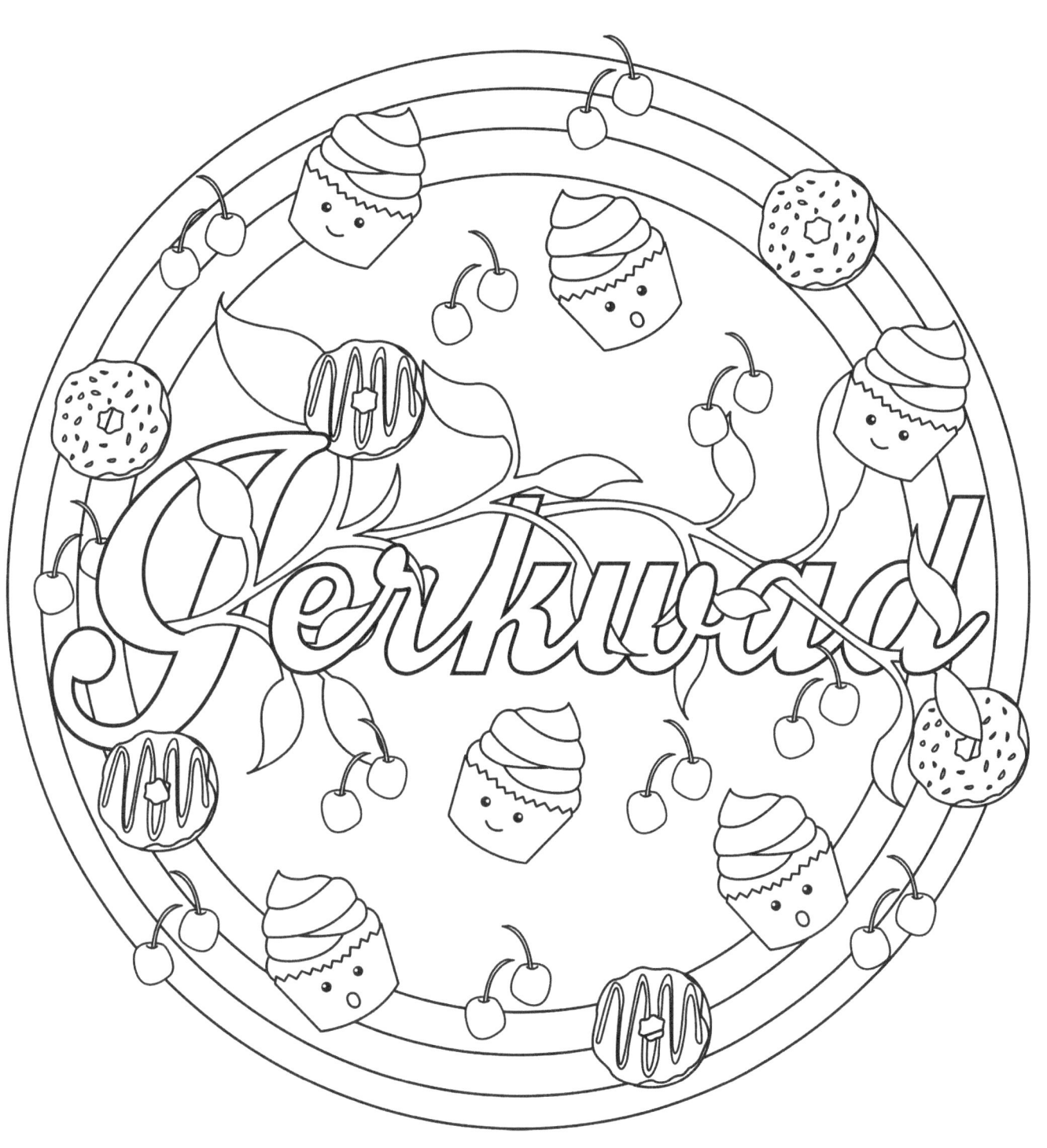

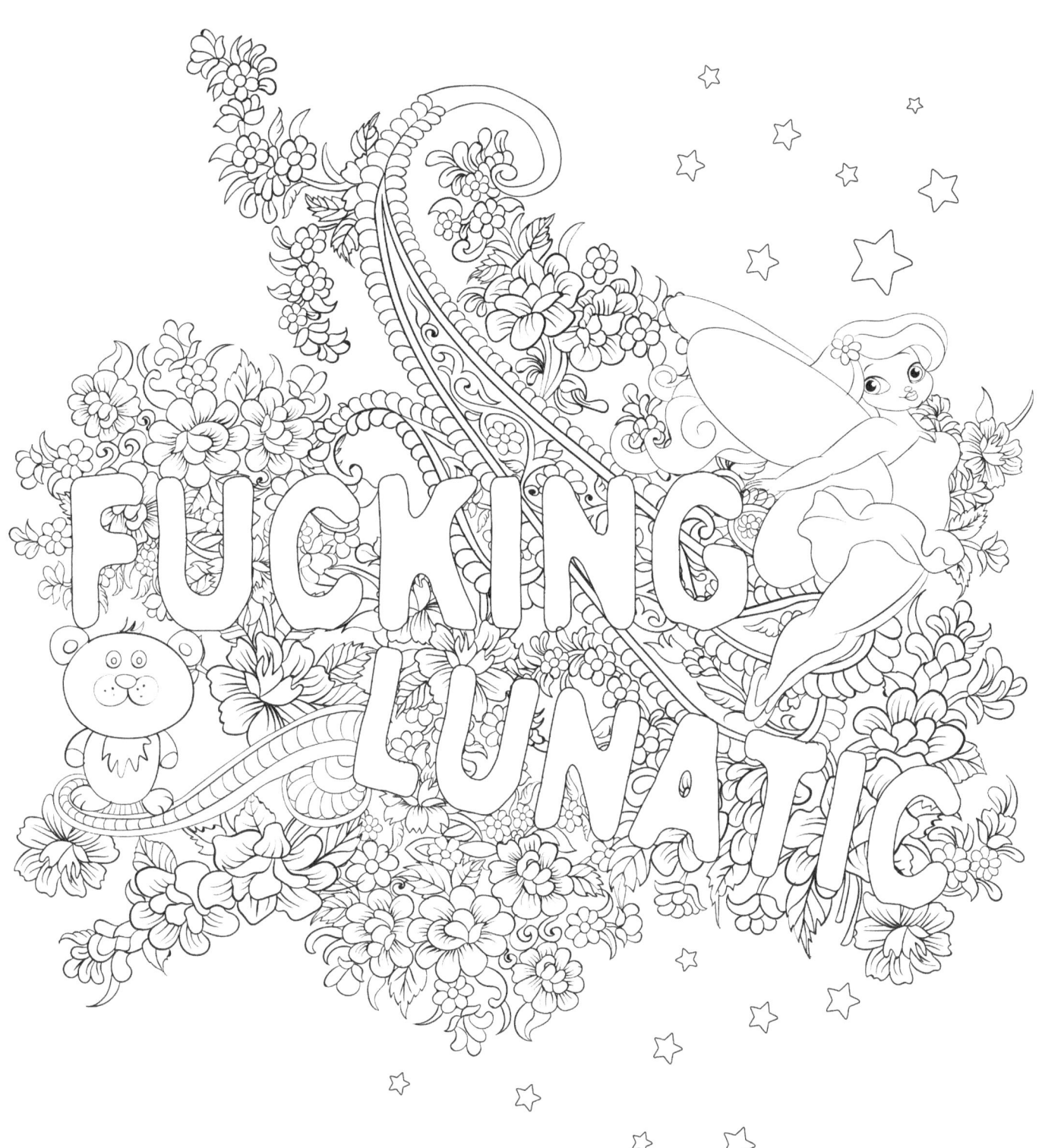

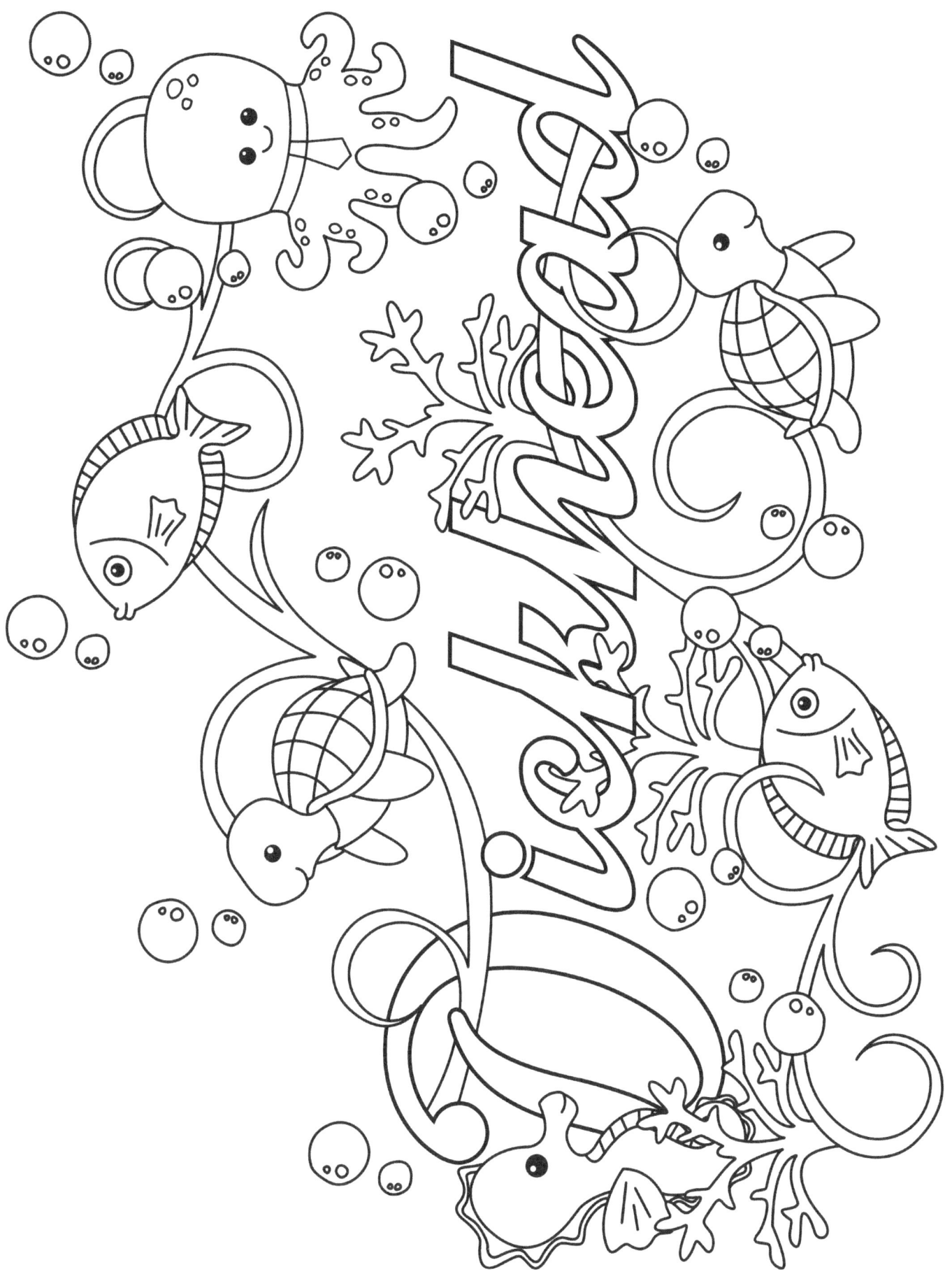

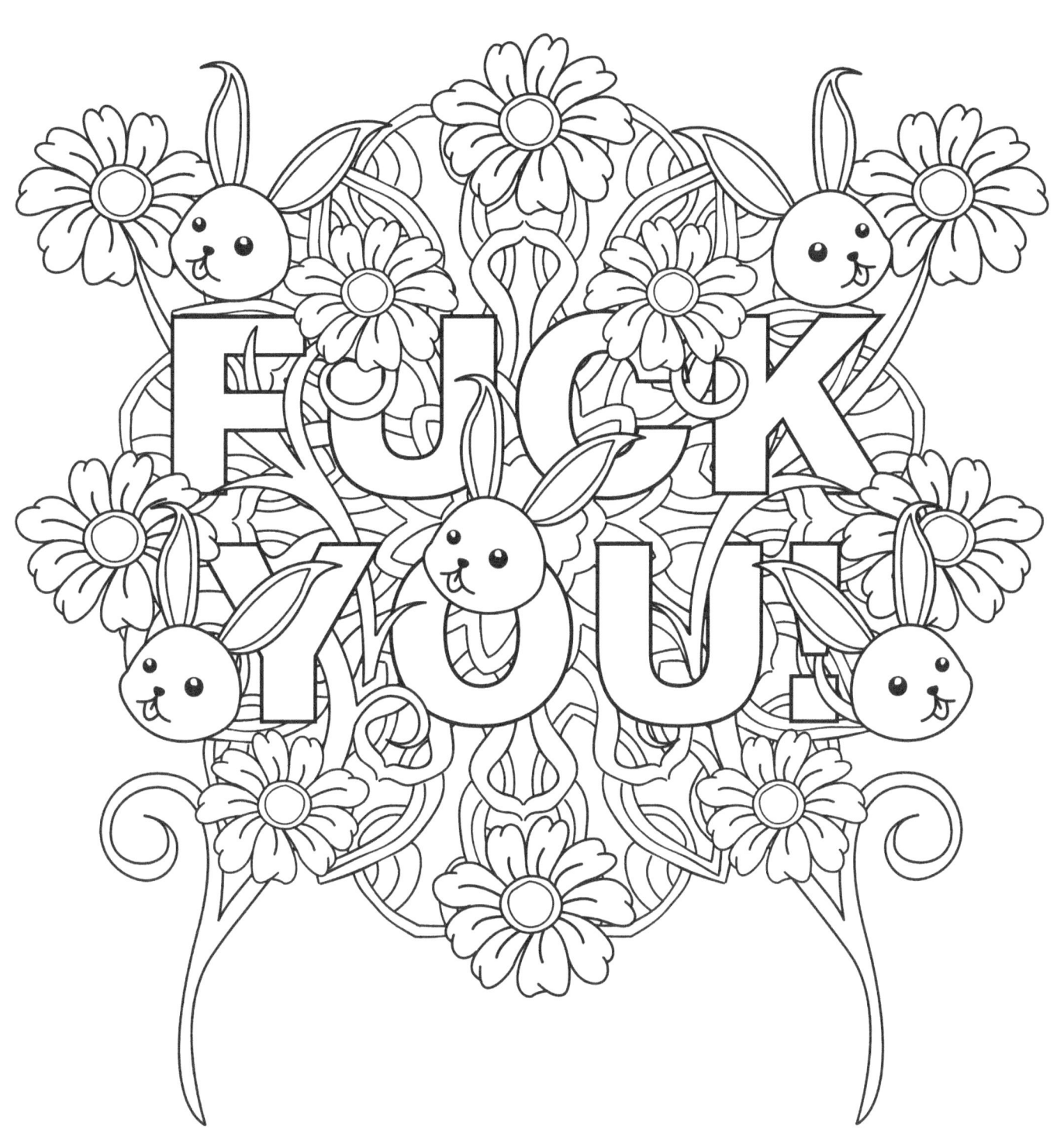

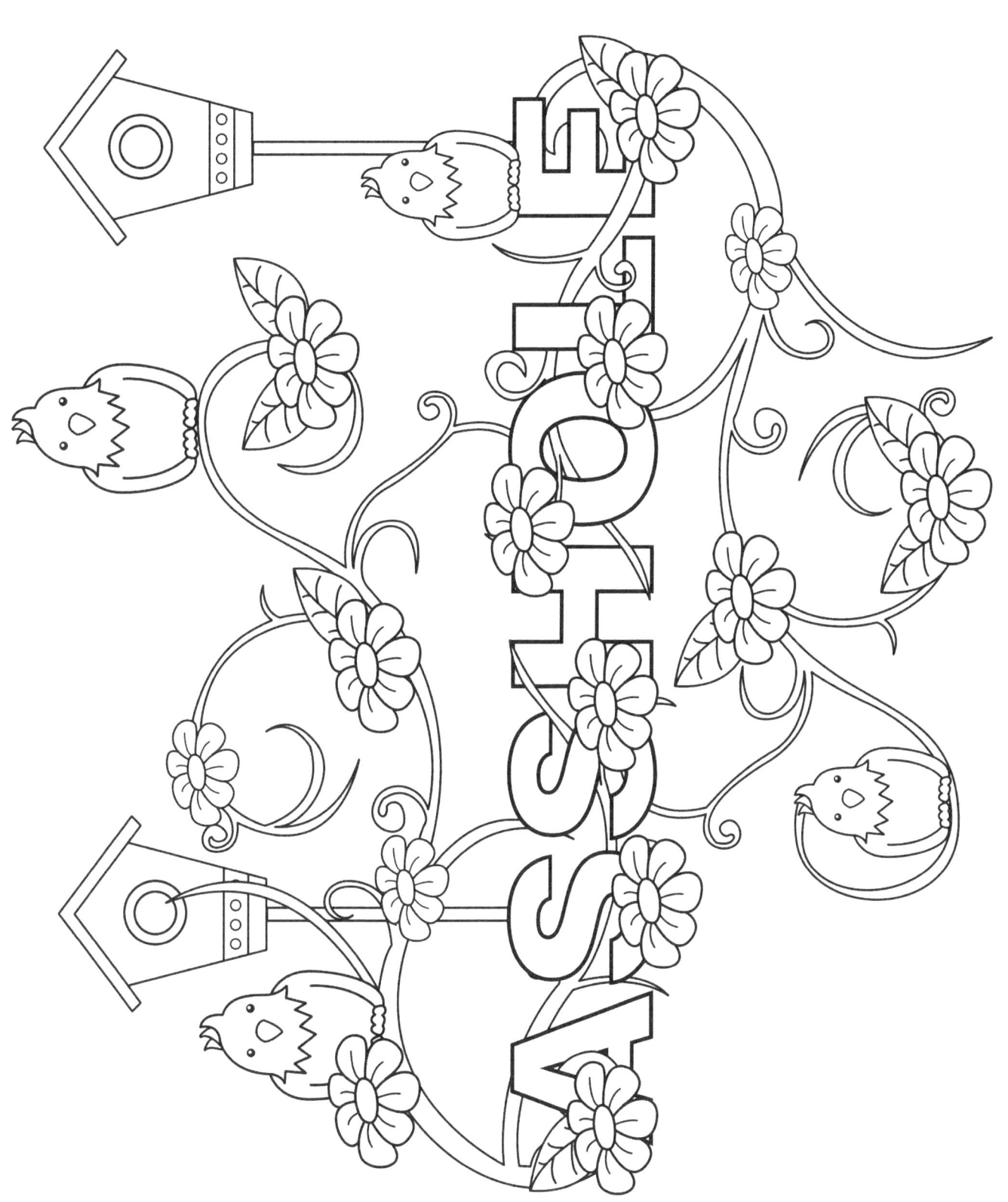

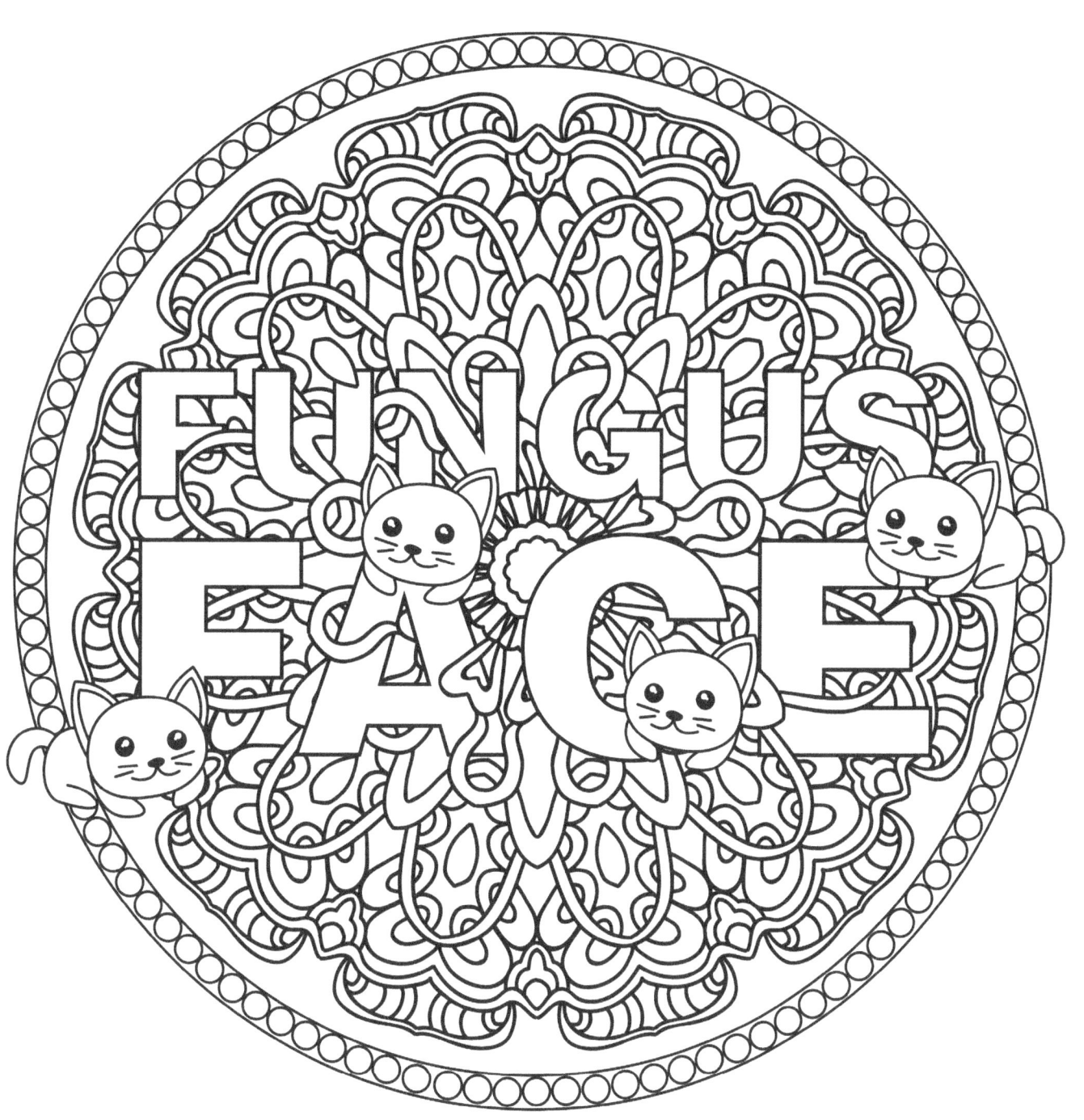

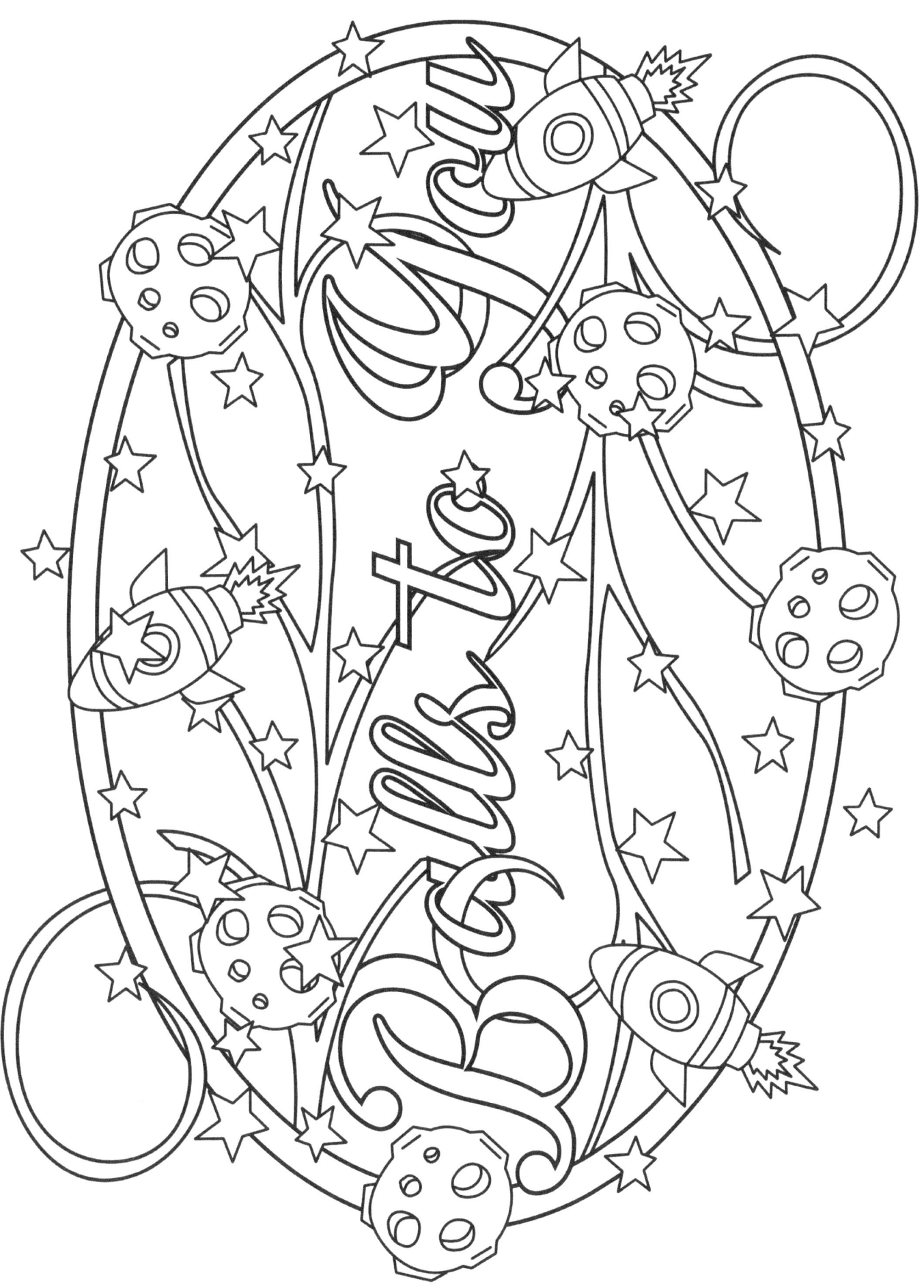

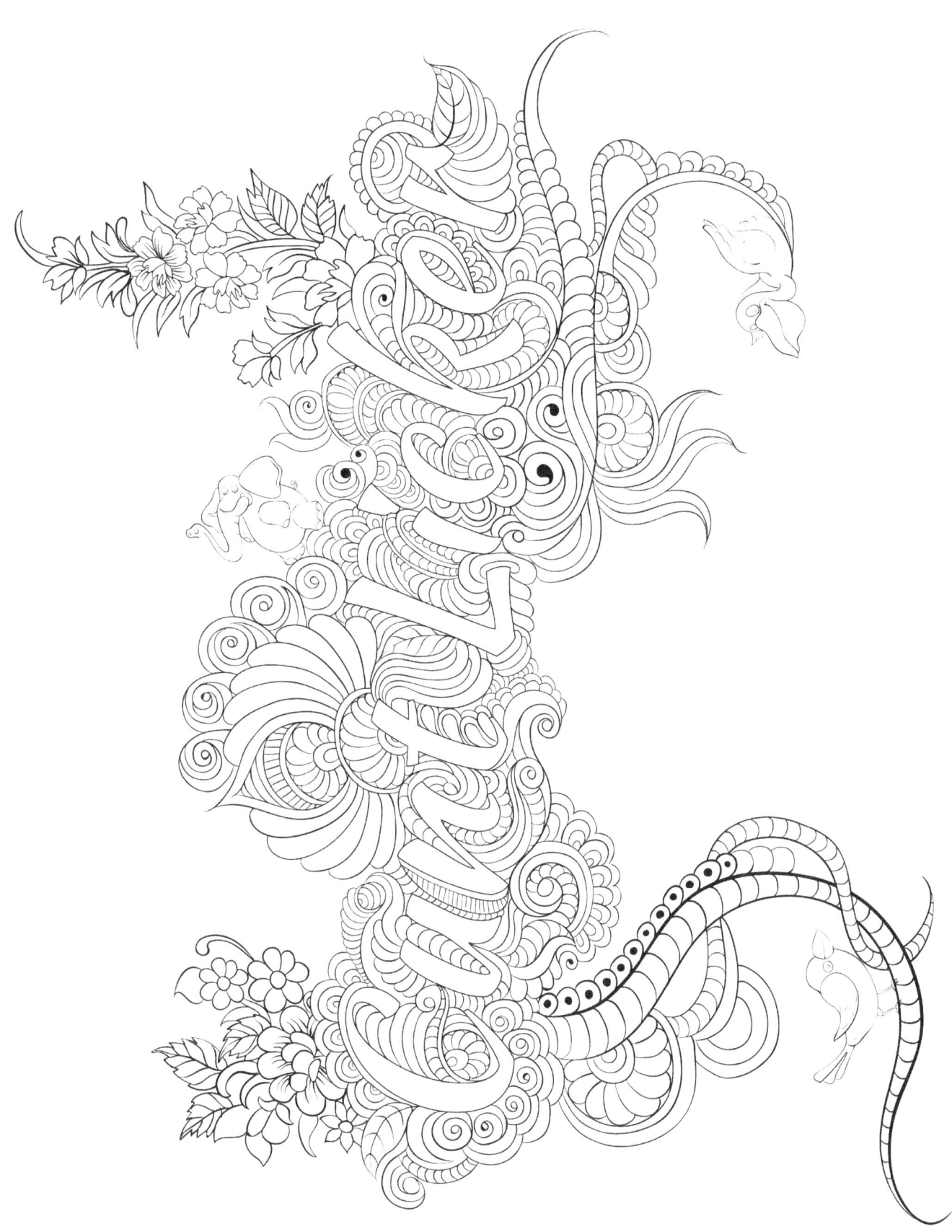

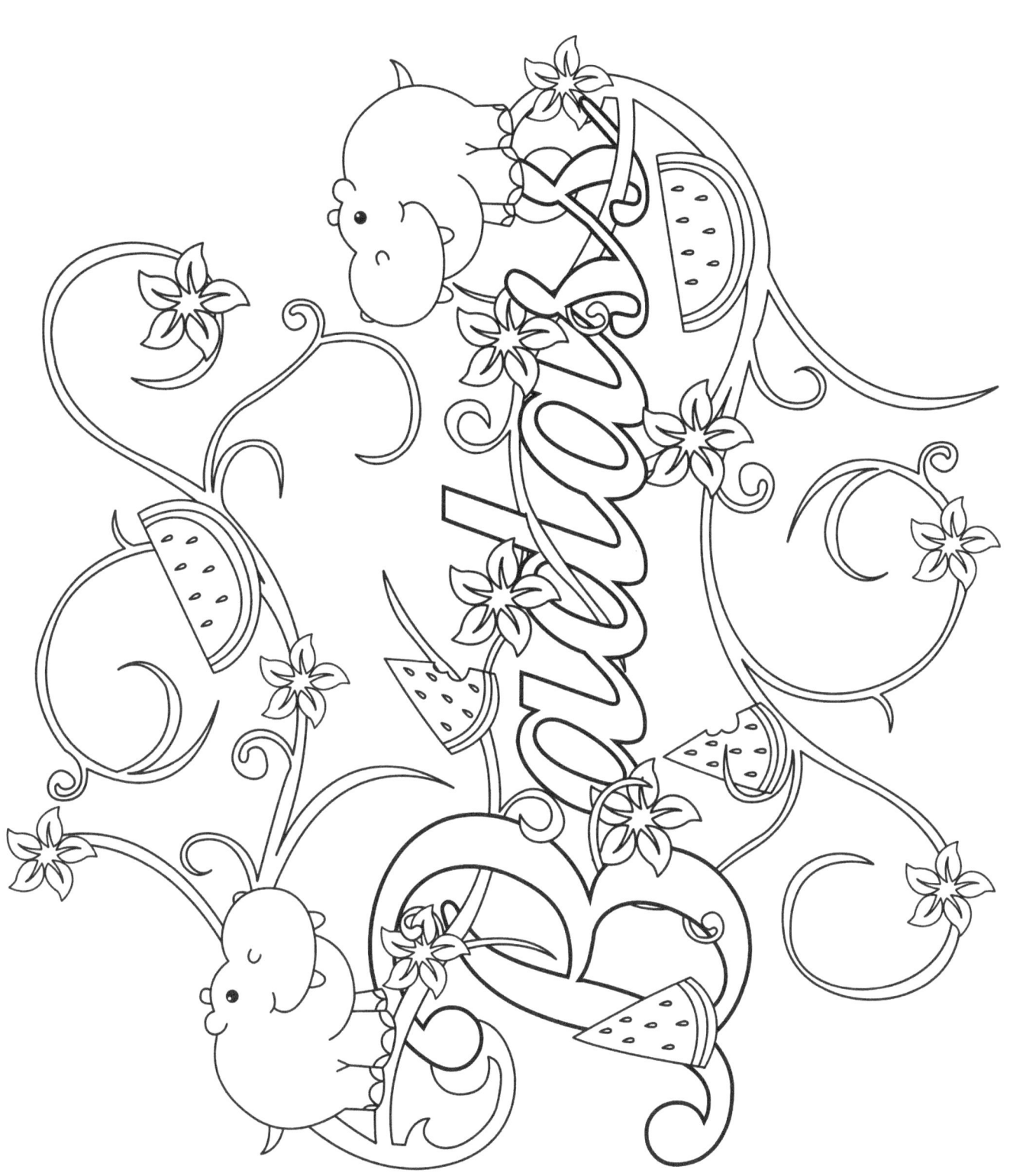

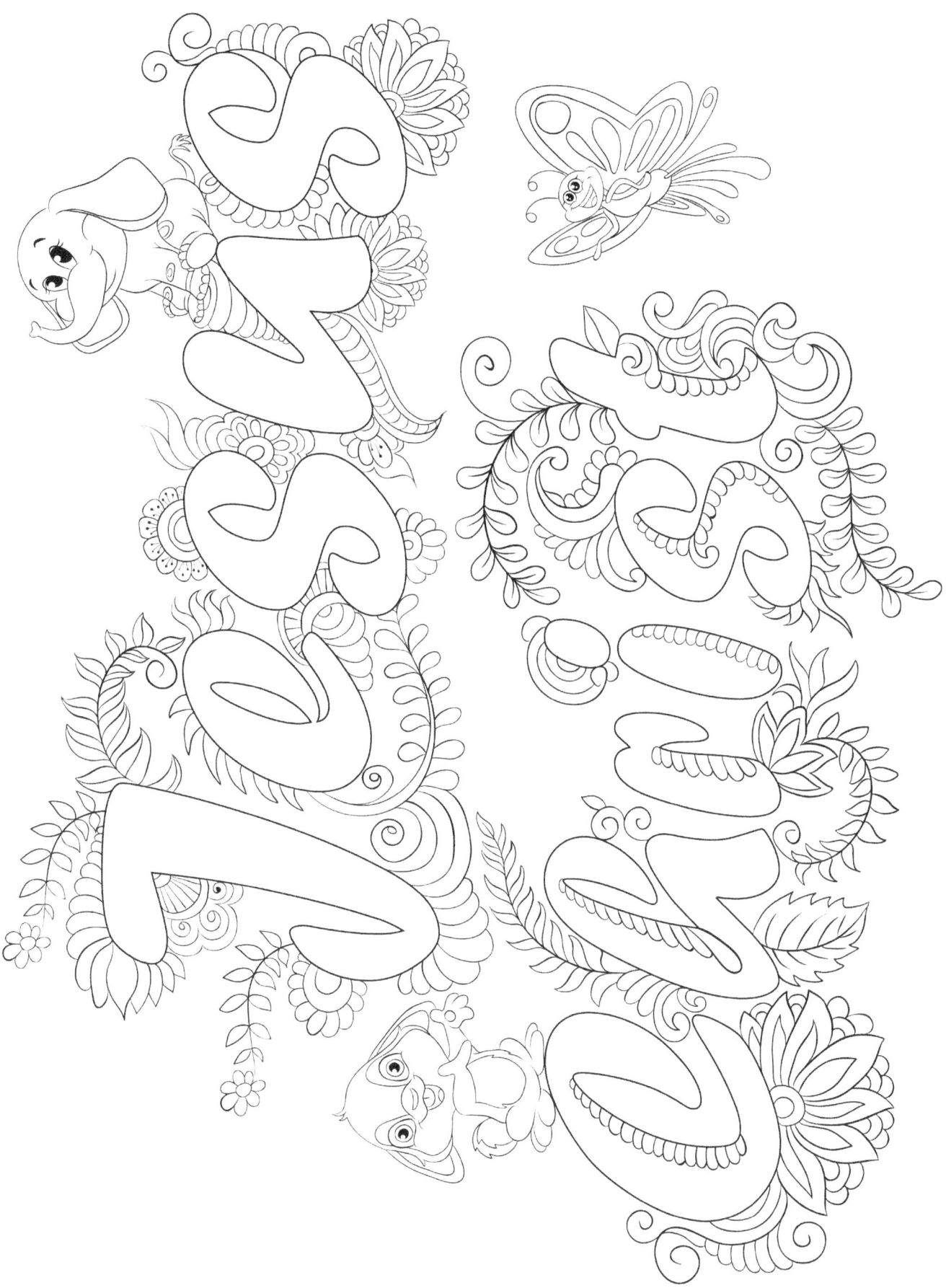

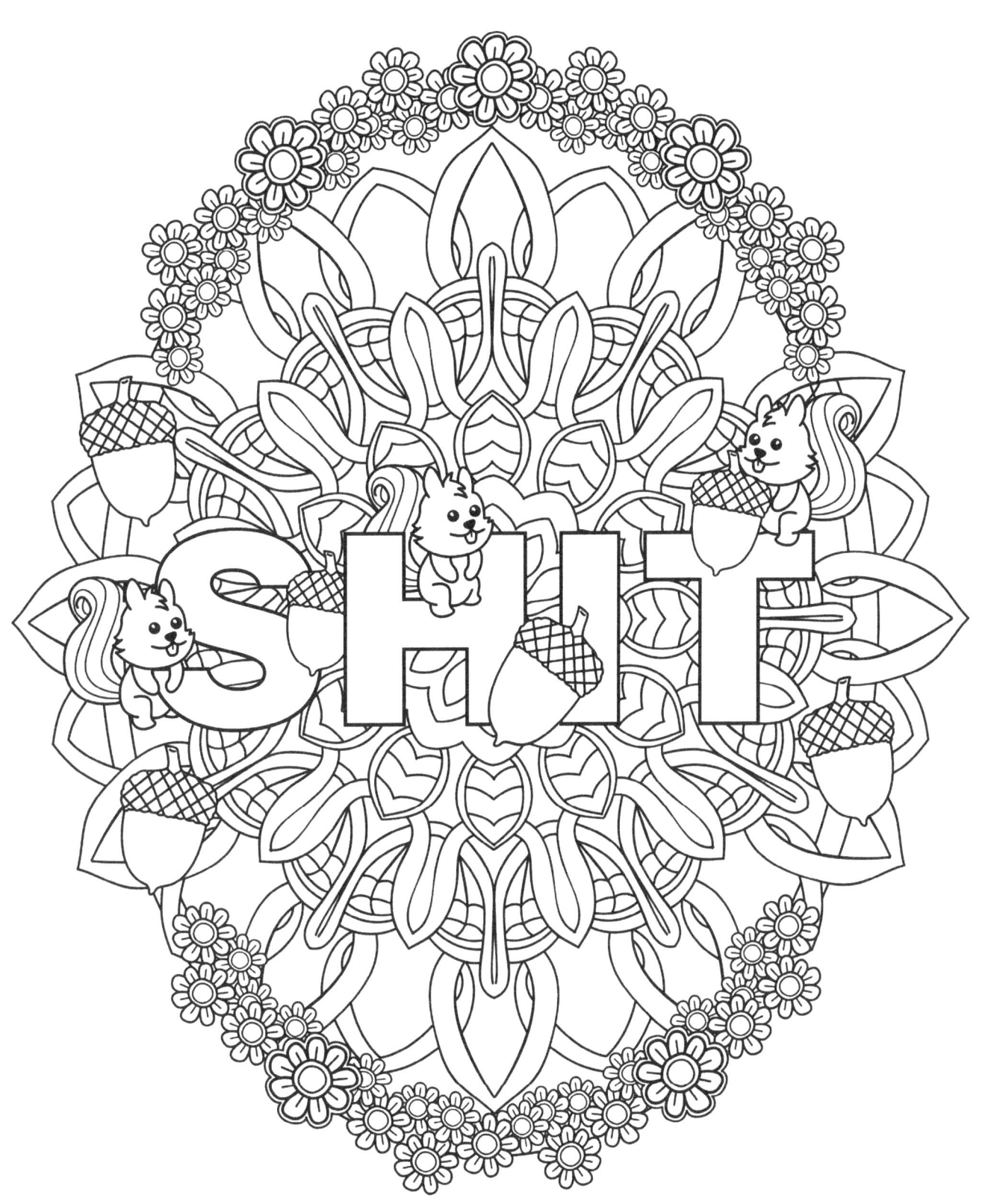

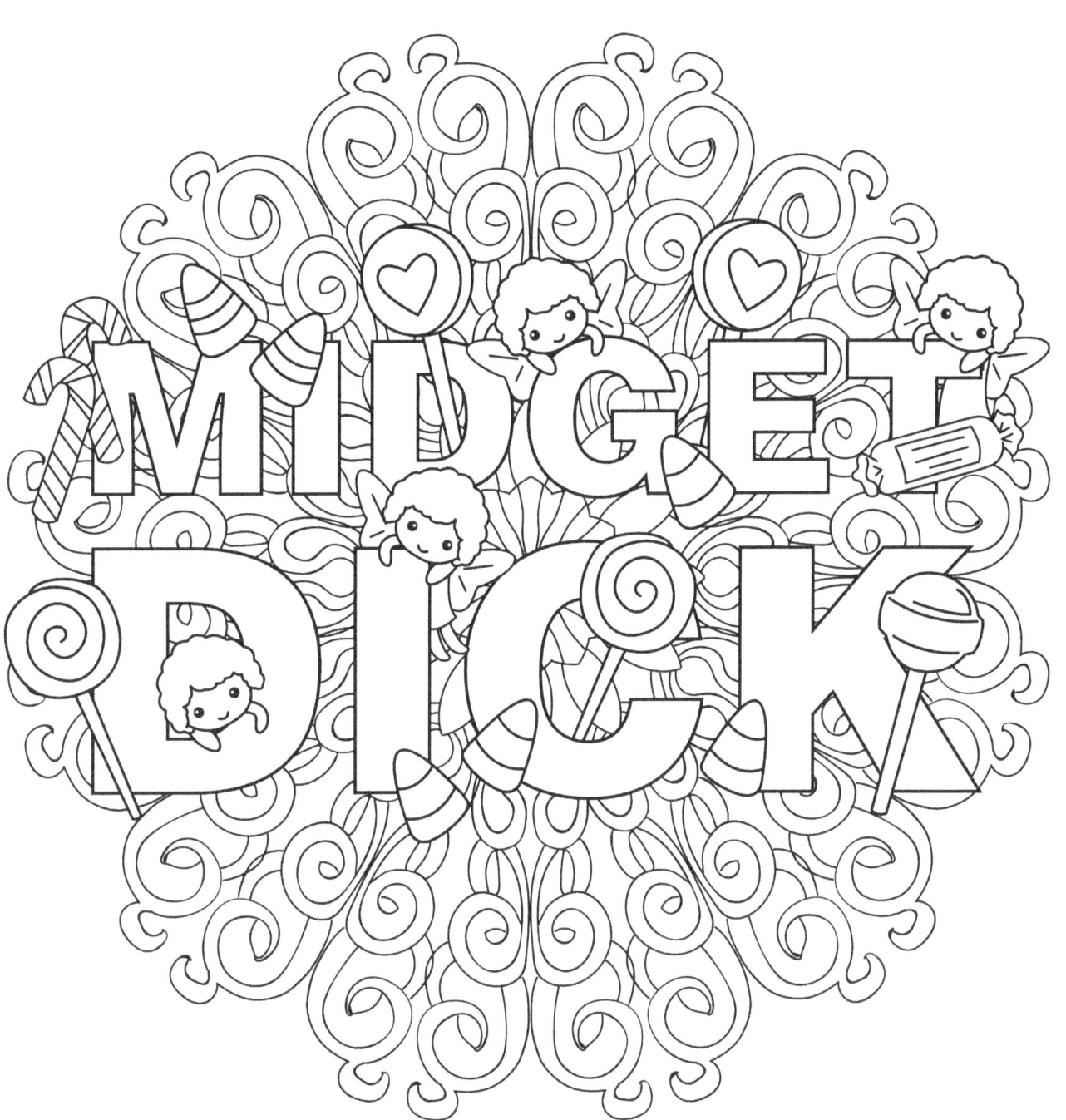

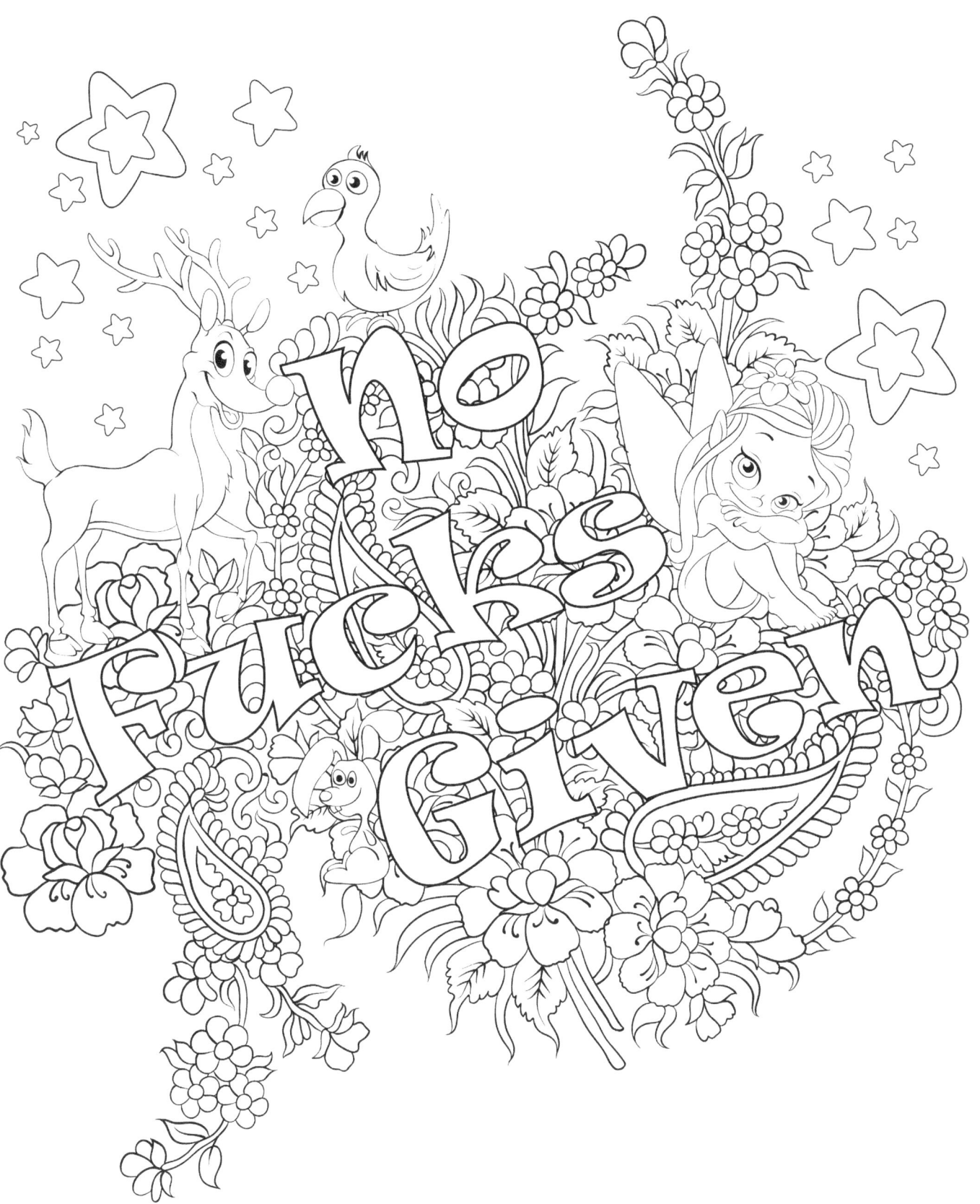

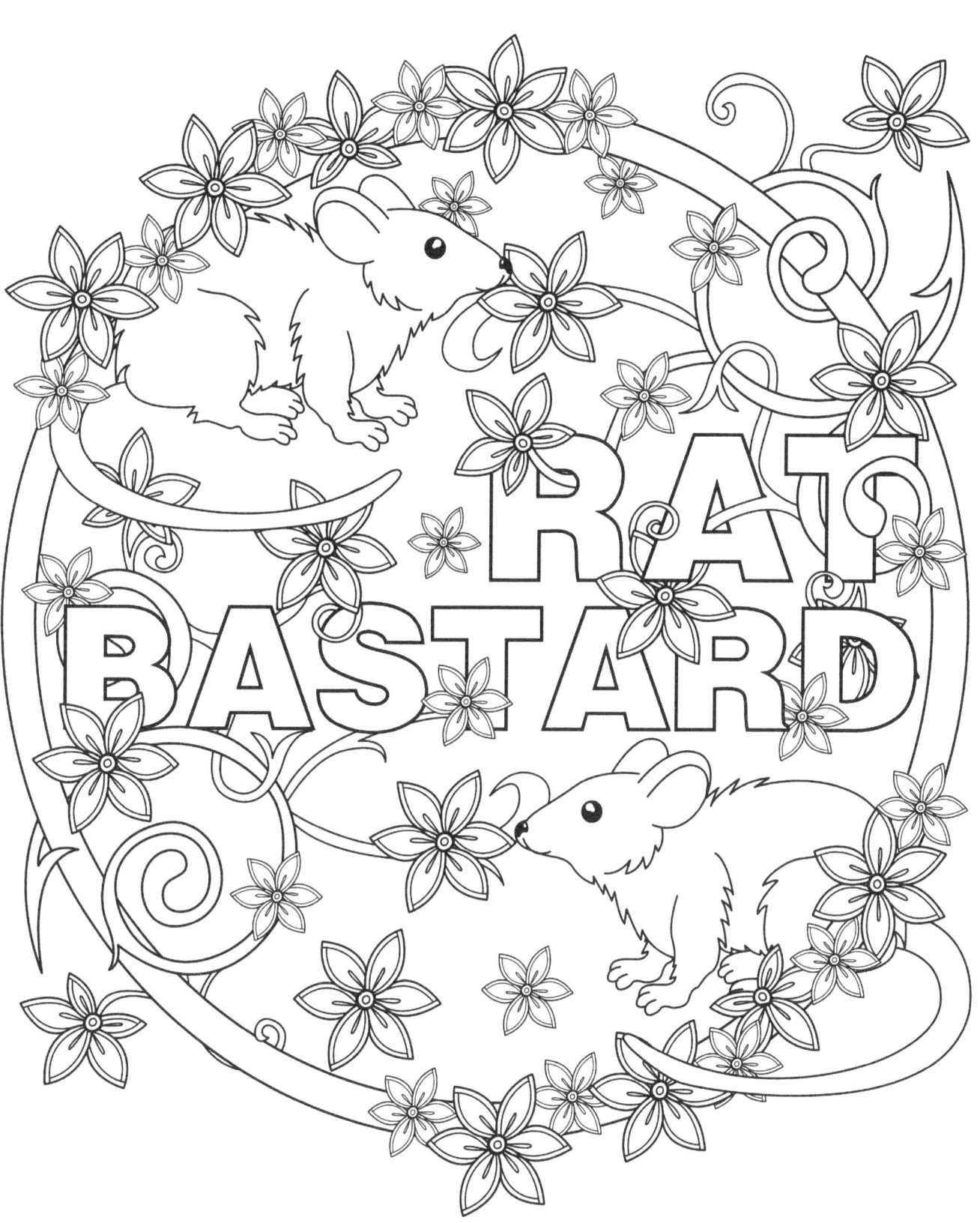

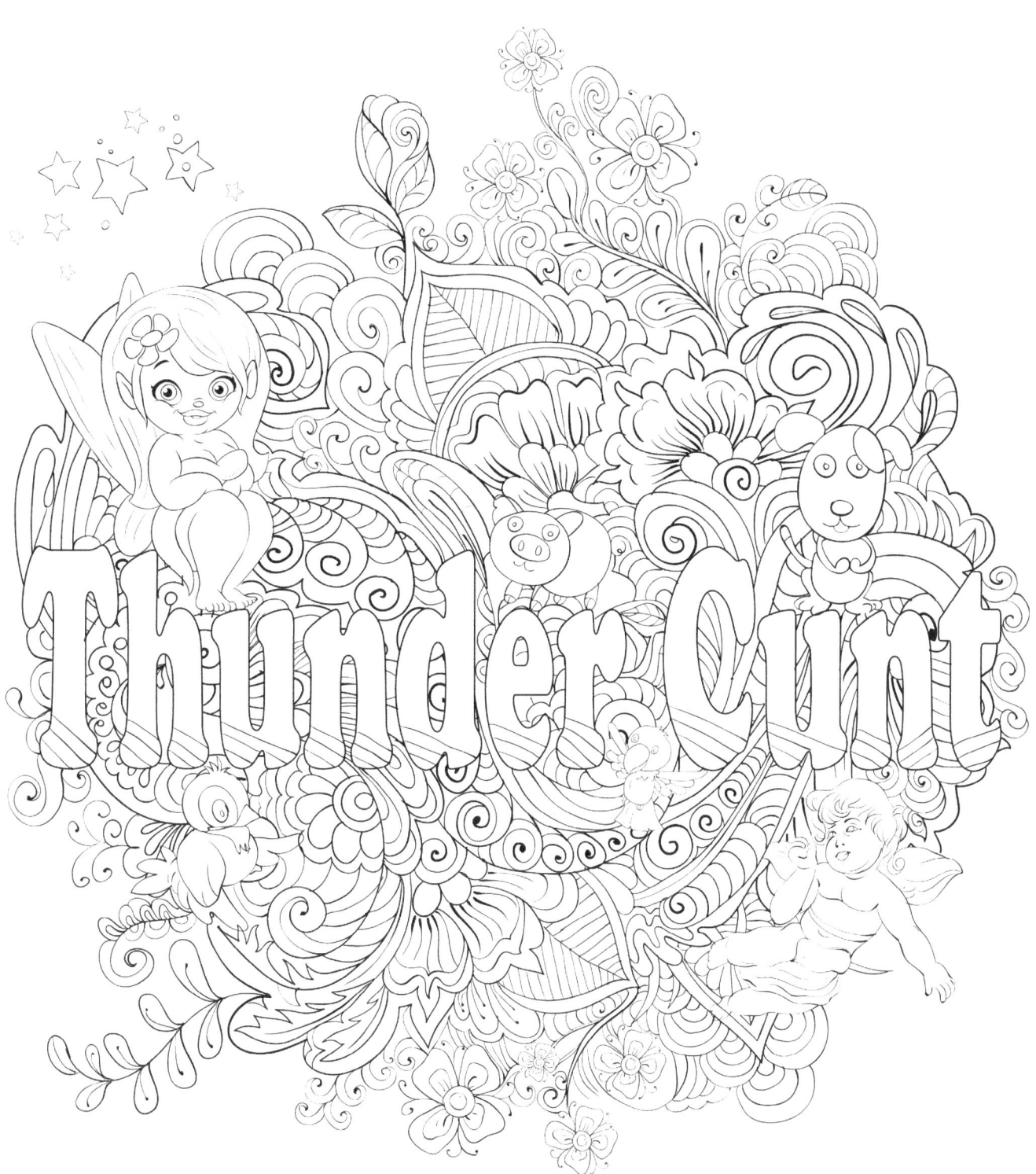

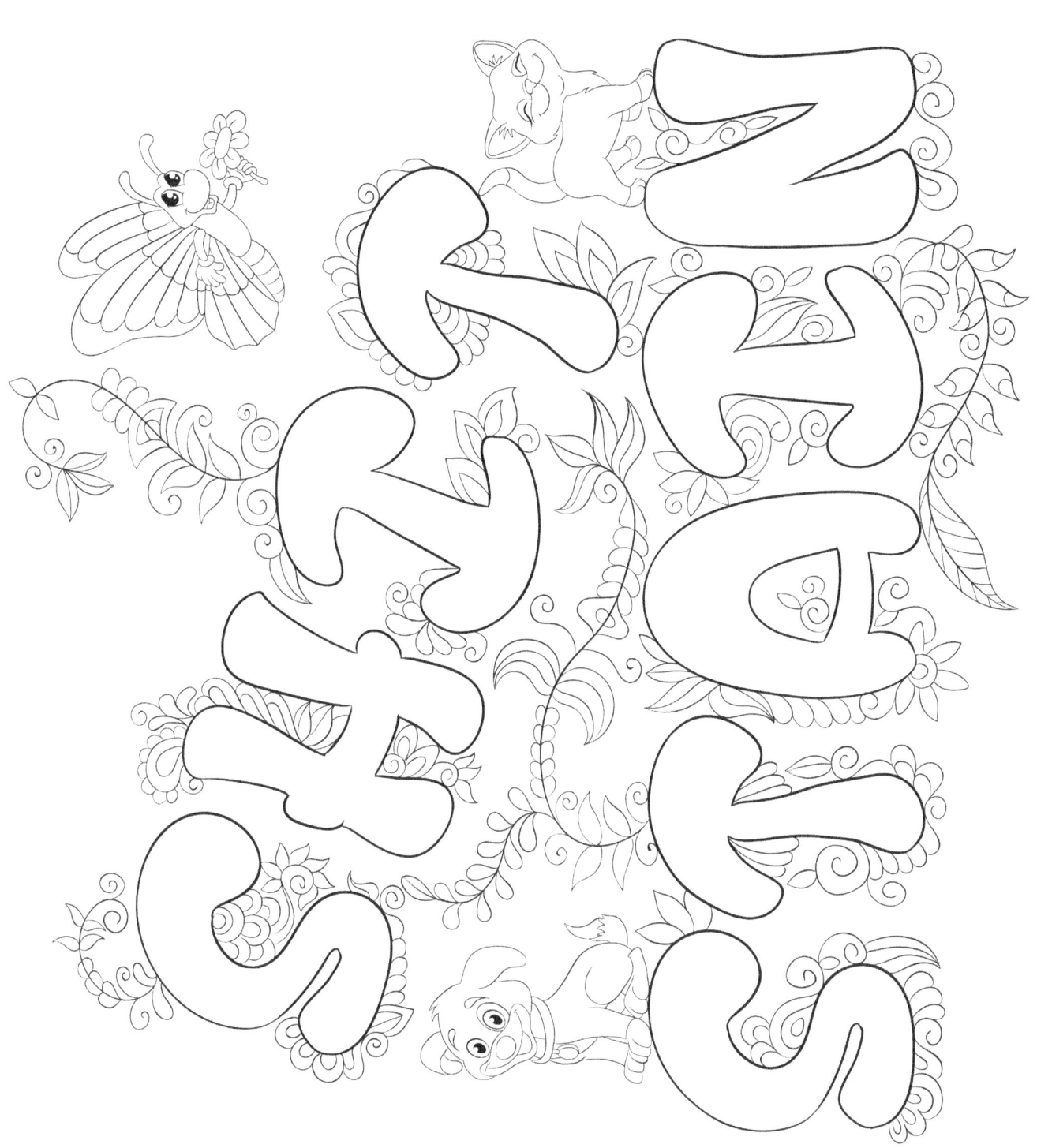

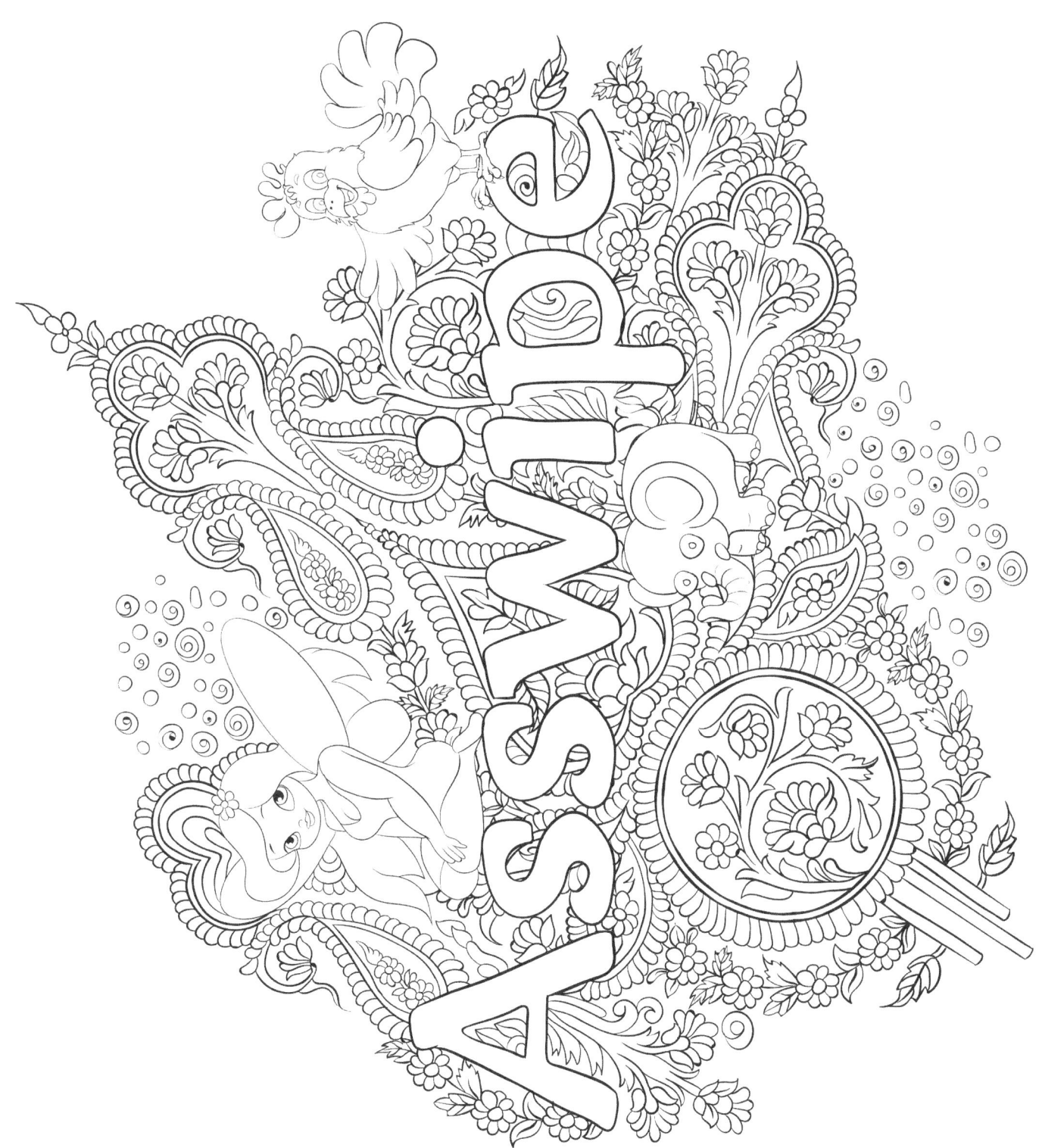

www.ingramcontent.com/pod-product-compliance
Lightning Source LLC
Chambersburg PA
CBHW080641190526
45169CB00009B/3453